meditations for walking

A little of trail wisdom may help us all. Don't try to do it all at once. Take breaks. Build leisure into your journey. Carry plenty of water and drink even when you don't think you are thirsty, because, if neglected, the springs of life within us can dry up without our even knowing it. Eat some of the food now; you need the nourishment, and besides, your pack won't be as heavy at journey's end. Watch your step, but more important, stop often and enjoy the view. God is here. *Kairos* meets *chronos* now. Each moment is holy. All time is God's.

—Jean Blomquist
"Holy Time, Holy Timing"
The Weavings Reader

meditations for walking

J. Lynne Hinton

Dot,

Thank you for
your support over
the years we have
known each other.
Your faith and
journey means a
great deal to many
people in your
community.
   May God continue
to grant you
peace on your
journey!
         Love,
         Lynne
         5/99

Smyth & Helwys Publishing, Inc.
Macon, Georgia

Smyth & Helwys Publishing, Inc.
6316 Peake Road
Macon, Georgia 31210-3960
1-800-747-3016
©1999 by Smyth & Helwys Publishing
All right reserved.
Printed in the United States of America.

J. Lynne Hinton

The paper used in this publication meets the minimum
requirements of American National Standard for Information
Sciences—Permanence of Paper for Printed Library
Materials.
ANSI Z39.48–1984. (alk. paper)

Library of Congress Cataloging-in-Publication Data

Hinton, J. Lynne.
    Meditations for walking / J. Lynne Hinton.
    pp.   cm.
    1. Meditations.
    I. Title.
    BV4832.2.H57   1999
    291.4'32—dc21   98-50648
                                                    CIP

ISBN 1-57312-264-5

*A portion of the proceeds of this book goes to Franklinton Center at Bricks.

For Bob, who always believed

Contents

Preface

Summer

The Beginning

Autumn

The Middle Passage

Winter

Deep into the Woods

Spring

Signs of New Life

Preface

For eight months I have been building a path in our back-
yard. Rows of pine trees frame our little house; and for the
seven years we have lived here, we have tried to clean out
the vines and underbrush that grow around and beside the
planted trees. We have not been very successful at a complete clearing. So I decided to wind a path through the
trees, back and forth along the edges and deep within the
forest that marks our property. It is a path through the
fallen timber, the twisting and poisonous vines, the deep
and layered stacks of leaves and pine straw and sticks. It is
a line through this forest we could not clean. Now as I walk
the pristine journey that stretches through the wildness of
outdoor life, I am convinced of the similarities between
this path and the paths our lives take both spiritually and
emotionally.

I like the metaphorical feel of walking through the forest on a path that was built primarily through a sense of
leading and intuition of how it should move. I often spoke
with my spiritual director about the path and how building
it or unbuilding it seemed so strangely in line and familiar
with the twists and turns and underbrush I face in my
spiritual life. Indeed, they speak of similar themes.

There were several storms leaving debris that cluttered
my path, at least one incident of having to return and start
over after the beginning had been destroyed, and many
moments of *deja vu* when the ground was too hard, the
vines too messy, the thorn bushes too numerous. There was
more than one occasion when I would stop to cry at the
futility of my work, sit to rest and take in the sounds and
sights around me. And there were many times when I
would question why the path would seemingly need to
wind in a certain direction when I felt quite confident that
I might find a better or faster way.

I learned about choices and patience. I struggled with poison ivy more than once. I recognized stubbornness and arrogance and the clean and satisfying feel of an easy rain. Now as I walk the path, still bending to clear and wipe away the previous night's clutter, I am made aware of the sacredness of this path that chose me and all the lessons I have learned.

I hope that, whether you are building your own path, walking lightly upon paths set before you, or just trying to find your way through the frightening and dense forest, this book might be a helpful signpost for your journey. My chosen path of Christianity may not be the spiritual path you are taking. I hope that doesn't diminish what this book or its quotations or Scripture passages can mean for your life.

Use the meditations as you like, as a way to begin your walking exercise, as a focus to maintain during the week, or as a guide to journal your thoughts and prayers. I hope the path I have taken can somehow assist you as you walk your own path. Remember that even though the way may seem narrow or treacherous, or even if the poison seems too threatening or the stones too sharp, you are never required nor expected to be completely alone.

Summer

the beginning

$\mathcal{S}$tarting the $\mathcal{P}$ath

*A voice cries out: "In the wilderness prepare the
way of the Lord, make straight in the desert a
highway for our God. Every valley shall be lifted
up, and every mountain and hill be made low; the
uneven ground shall become level, and the rough
places a plain. Then the glory of the Lord shall be
revealed, and all people shall see it together, for
the mouth of the Lord has spoken." (Isaiah 40:3-5)*

Today I begin. Unsure of where the path should start, I
walked around the edge of the forest from end to end. How
will I know the best place to begin raking away the tangles? It is a vast area to consider a journey. I had not
thought it would be so difficult to know how to begin.

Today I waited with a family at the hospital for information regarding their loved one. The diagnosis had been
feared and dreaded. We sat together in silence as the doc-
tor described the discovery of lung cancer and a surgery
that was only somewhat successful. His words hung above
us like the air in summer. After a few minutes of waiting for
questions that had no time to be formed, he backed away
from the room, leaving the family alone with their pain.

I knew that rarely are there appropriate words on such
an occasion. As I had become accustomed to doing, I
shifted and yanked, pulled into and away from my helplessness. It was an awkward and difficult pause in the busy
normalcy of our lives. As I sat with the family, without any
necessary means of comfort, I was drawn to the notion of
the path and where it should begin.

When I arrived home and stood at the edge, I realized
that perhaps my sign had come in the hospital waiting

room. Lost in the silence of someone else's suffering without the right words was the starting place for which I had searched. It was nothing more than my helplessness.

Perhaps this feeling, this struggle, is the most human, least egotistical, clearest sign of a beginning I would find. Because in my helplessness, I recognize I cannot uncover the path alone. I must have guidance and grace. I must begin by understanding this is not my path, in that I have chosen it and will build it. This is not a path that will come about because of my good doing. This is not my path alone.

The paths we take begin before we make the decision to follow them. The journey happens when we aren't even paying attention. And there is something very humbling but also reassuring in knowing that it begins without any action on our part. It begins when we are helpless.

A recently planted snowball bush grows just at the edge of the pine tree forest. It seems somehow dwarfed by the large pines all around it; but because it seems set apart, isolated, even out of place, it makes a nice place to start. Here is where my chosen path begins. The new path curves to the left, heads into the rambles and brambles of a forest, and then quickly turns right, between two trees. I stop. I have come far enough. I have found a beginning.

Meditation for Walking

How do you describe the beginning of your spiritual path? How is helplessness integrated into your journey?

Prayer for Walking

God, Maker of this path I walk, open my eyes to see how to begin to walk each day with you. Amen.

Week 2

Walking in the Midst of Trouble

Though I walk in the midst of trouble, you pre-
serve me against the wrath of my enemies; you
stretch out your hand, and your right hand deliv-
ers me. The Lord will fulfill his purpose for me;
your steadfast love, O Lord, endures forever. Do
not forsake the work of your hands. (Psalm 138:7-
8)

Previously I stopped my work on the path just as it had
come upon a small sapling right in the center of where the
path was heading. Today as I continue, I must decide what
to do about the young tree. I must choose whether to uproot the sapling, moving it out of my way, or find a means
to include it on the path.

In our spiritual lives we stumble over the unexpected.
Recently I had lunch with a young couple who was planning their wedding. Our time together was limited since
the bridegroom had an afternoon radiation treatment and
his initial assessment with Hospice. The talk was strained
cheerfulness, but we managed a few decisions including
that the service should be held during a Sunday morning
worship so that the entire church could share in this
celebration of commitment.

Ronnie and Peggy are walking straight towards trouble.
With a diagnosis of metastatic melanoma, they have heard
the grave prognosis and understand what is more than
likely ahead for them. Yet they have decided to make a
commitment to each other in the midst of this bad news,
this tragedy that sits dead center in their way. This trouble
that has sprung up on their path will not and cannot deter
them from the direction they would walk together. It might

5

slow them down and alter things a bit, but it cannot shrink their love for each other or undermine the life they intend to share together. It will not stop the path.

The Psalmist writes about walking in the midst of trouble; and I think about Peggy and Ronnie and their decision to face what lies ahead of them, together. Choosing to commit oneself to another is no easy choice. When the stakes are as high as radiation treatments and cancer and a poor prognosis, the commitment to continue seems even more unlikely. Yet the Psalmist reminds us that even though we might walk in the midst of travail or great trouble, the path itself, our lives will be preserved; that our paths, which are filled with the loves and promises we are blessed enough to find, will be completed with a fulfilled purpose for our living. This is the greatest news for me to uncover. The purpose for my life, for my living will be fulfilled.

Today in the clearing the path widened to make room for the young pine sapling. The path grew and then came back together. I placed stones and twigs around the little tree, realizing that it has its place on the path. Not always do we walk "over." Not always is it necessary to "uproot." There are times and places on our paths when we allow what is there to stay, unchanged and untouched. We learn from it without having to dissect it. We simply let it be.

Meditation for Walking

What is the trouble in your midst? How can you widen your path to include this "trouble"?

Prayer for Walking

Give me grace and wisdom to recognize the trouble that in the midst I need to walk. Amen.

The Risk of Creation

In the beginning when God created the heavens and the earth, the earth was a formless void and darkness covered the face of the deep, while a wind from God swept over the face of the waters. (Genesis 1:1-2)

I look over my path's meager beginnings and ponder the thoughts of God at the creation of the earth. How must it have felt to God watching as the light separated from the darkness, as earth moved out of heaven, water from land? How did it feel observing plants and lights and birds and fish and all kinds of creatures stepping out and about this new thing that emerged from God's heart? I wonder if there was a moment of sadness for God or hesitation at the realization that nothing would ever be the same again.

Steps taken in faith create for us new paths that render our lives different from the ones we lived before. Though we may fall back and regress and return, we can never go completely back to the life we previously lived. Because once we step out in faith, once we begin to create and to be created, we are changed in a way that keeps us from being able to go back to an earlier existence of ignorance.

There are risks in walking a path of faith. There is the risk that we will lose something to which we held tightly and the risk that those who have walked with us will not choose to walk with us now. God, as Creator, took a great risk in setting the universe into motion. Perhaps God's greatest risk was the creation of humankind. Surely we have left God disappointed and even regretful because of our sinful ways.

Yet we can be sure that God continues to love and care for God's creation, even and maybe even especially the creation of humankind. It was a risk taken in love and a risk God continues to honor.

Even though the path may have gone differently than even God imagined, God continued to allow the path of creation to move forward. Even in God's anger at the poor and sinful choices of humankind, God repented and allowed the world to keep turning. Creation is God's greatest risk, evidence of so great a love.

We must remember in our own lives that once we take that first step, we can change paths or quit walking; but we can never really go back to the way we once were. We are changed forever by the risks we have taken. Allowing God to create in and through us permits the possibility of disappointment and rejection; but it also opens us to unimagined beauty.

Let us pray that we can continue to walk in faith.

Meditation for Walking

What risks do you take in living a life of faith? What is being created in your life as a result of faith?

Prayer for Walking

Today as I walk this path of faith, create in me a clean and right heart that new things may begin in me. Amen.

Dwelling in the Vine

I am the true vine, and my Father is the vine-grower. He removes every branch in me that bears no fruit. Every branch that bears fruit he prunes to make it bear more fruit. You have already been cleansed by the word that I have spoken to you. Abide in me as I abide in you. Just as the branch cannot bear fruit by itself unless it abides in the vine, neither can you unless you abide in me. I am the vine, you are the branches. Those who abide in me and I in them bear much fruit, because apart from me you can do nothing. Whoever does not abide in me is thrown away like a branch and withers; such branches are gathered, thrown into the fire, and burned. (John 15:1-6)

There are lots of vines along this path. It is like a tangled mess. I tug and pull, yank and cut. But still, if I dig beneath the surface of the ground, down below straw and soil, I can always unearth the roots of some vine. I have noticed in this work that the farther away from the root the vine grows, the weaker it becomes and the easier it is to pull it away. But those vines closest to the root are impossible to tear away or break.

As branches, we grow from the vine that is the source of our spirit. When we creep farther and farther away from the root, the source, the center of our spirits, the weaker our faith becomes and the easier it is to pull us away from our source.

Sometimes in moving away from our center, our root, we twist and turn about the wrong tree, tangling ourselves in concerns and business that are not ours to fear nor ours in which we need to be engaged. We become distracted and confused. And we wither under that strength of other vines and roots.

Today the path moved more deeply into the forest. The ground is busier, the obstacles more numerous. It is hard and slow work to move ahead. I wrestle with the vines. And yet, straight down into the heart of the woods, then with a turn to the right, the journey continues.

Meditation for Walking

Are you dwelling in the vine? In what places of your life are you trying to bear fruit alone? What aspects of your life seem withered?

Prayer for Walking

Graft me, O God, into the true vine. For here is the source of all I will ever need. Let me dwell in thee. Amen.

The Source of Me

*O Lord, you have searched me and known me.
You know when I sit down and when I rise up;
you discern my thoughts from far away. You
search out my path and my lying down, and are
acquainted with all my ways. (Psalm 139:1-3)*

I lift up my eyes
to tops of trees
and wind-blown clouds

Who speaks my name?
Who knows my secrets and
still loves me?

God of Heaven
God of earth
God of saints
but mostly sinners
of children
of aged and wrinkled folks
of tiny, tiny creatures
and sea monsters
and green, green leaves

I drop my eyes
to dirt and stones
wiggling toes in dust

Who has a finger on the
pulsing of my sad heart?
Who catches my smile in the
corner of their eye?

God of worlds here and beyond
God of angels and lizards
and breathing beds of rivers
of trunks of trees and seeds that fly
of morning and star
and pitch black of night
and me

Great, holy God
of me.

Meditation for Walking

Write your own poem or psalm about who God is
for you. Let nature inform your thoughts.

Prayer for Walking

You are my beginning and my end, the source of all
that is me. Let me abide in you forever. Amen.

Seeing Dimly

Love never ends. But as for prophecies, they will come to an end; as for tongues, they will cease; as for knowledge, it will come to an end.... For now we see in a mirror, dimly, but then we will see face to face. Now I know only in part; then I will know fully, even as I have been fully known. (1 Corinthians 13:8, 12)

Paul wrote these words just after having discussed the expectations and gift of love. Perhaps he understood, as he penned those words, the mystery of trying to live a life of love. Perhaps he understood the frustration of being unable to see into the future or know the reasons and purposes for certain relationships or events in our lives.

I look out into the forest that spreads before me, and I do not know the direction the path will take. I cannot see what will pass my way in the days to come. I cannot find the next clearing. I realize that a part of continuing on this journey is directly and concretely tied to hope and the promise that one day we will see all and understand fully all events and circumstances. One day we shall look back upon our paths and all the turns and twists they took, and it will be made clear to us, the purpose, the reasons. Paul does not explain how or when this will happen. He simply writes what has been placed on his heart and continues his thought process as it remains, in the context of love.

We are challenged to live our lives, walk our paths, based on love, a love that is patient and kind and not jealous or boastful or arrogant or rude, a love that bears and believes and hopes and endures all things. So that when we come to the end of our paths, because of the love we have been given, we will have the clear image of what the love meant.

Though I look out into the forest in which my journey goes and see nothing clearly, one day I will know where I have been going and where I have been.

Meditation for Walking

How do you handle knowing only in part? Are you able to trust that one day you will understand? How does love help you in following an unclear path?

Prayer for Walking

As I walk in love, let me trust that all that is blurred will one day be clear. Amen.

The Purses We Carry

Sell your possessions, and give alms. Make purses for yourselves that do not wear out, an unfailing treasure in heaven, where no thief comes near and no moth destroys. For where your treasure is, there your heart will be also. (Luke 12:33-34)

Recently I preached on this passage. I took a box full of my purses to the pulpit and talked about each one, where I got them, why I picked them out. Most of the purses I had in the box were large ones, good for carrying lots of things. "Here's the thing, though," I told the congregation, "it seems the larger my purse, the more stuff I carry in it; the more stuff I carry, the heavier the purse gets, and the weaker and more tired my shoulders and neck become."

It's true for all areas of our lives. The more we try to carry around with us, the more burdened we become. Try to walk your path with grudges and bitterness, chips on your shoulder, and you'll find yourself weighted down. Try to enjoy your walk when your arms are filled with all the things you think you must have, and you'll discover you don't feel much like moving. Step with too much baggage, and you'll soon decide not to go any further.

I carry a tiny little purse these days. I have to wrestle with what to do with my keys. I don't have any room for lipstick or tissues, but my load is lighter. I don't feel so tired and weighted down any more. And I'm not having to wade through a lot of unnecessary stuff, trying to find the thing I need.

In the same way, I pray as I walk my path, that I will lighten the load, that God will lighten the load for me. I understand that I may have become attached to the purse

I carry and that allowing the purse to be emptied may be quite painful. (There are always things I think I have to have.) But I also know that as long as I am worried with these purses and all the things I carry in them, I am unable to provide for myself a purse that does not grow old. As long as my heart is distracted and burdened by so many treasures, I am unable to claim the real treasure, walking lightly.

Meditation for Walking

What is the purse you carry? Is your walk burdensome because you are trying to carry too many things? What can you let go of to be able to walk lightly?

Prayer for Walking

Relieve me, O God, from those treasures that wear me down. Let me find my treasure, my heart, in you. Amen.

Week 8

Considering the Lilies

Consider the lilies of the field, how they grow; they neither toil nor spin. . . . Therefore do not worry, saying, "What will we eat?" or "What will we drink?" or "What will we wear?" . . . But strive first for the kingdom of God and his righteousness, and all these things will be given to you as well. (Matthew 6:28b, 31, 33)

There is life in this forest. Tiny pink flowers grow in the rays of sunshine that angle themselves between the heavy trunks of trees. They are like little hearts dangling from their green stems, fed by the earth and colored by the sun. They are not the lilies of the field about which Jesus spoke, but they remind me of his words since they neither toil nor spin and yet are arrayed so delicately and beautifully.

Why are we obsessed with worry or fear? Why can't we trust that God will provide us with all we need? Why do we fear we will not be cared for, and thereby create unnecessary anxiety for ourselves? Why do we tend to value ourselves and others by the way we look, the way we dress, the amount of money we spend on our clothes?

As I walk through these woods, slowly and deliberately, I am awakened to real beauty. I am ashamed by my society-shaped ideals of what is beautiful. I am aware of how easy it is to be swayed by cultural beauty myths.

Jesus reminds us that the flowers are true beauty, that the flowers do not work or worry about their worth or their appearance. They do not toil nor spin. They simply are. In all their glory and splendor, they just are.

God provides for them; and if God provides for them, then surely God will provide for us. We need not be anxious about anything. Just look around. Notice all that has been taken care of. Then believe. God will provide.

Meditation for Walking

What aspects of your life worry you most? Are you able to put all things aside and seek first God's kingdom? Ask God to help you find your inner beauty and to let go of your need to be accepted by your appearance.

Prayer for Walking

I am a flower created by you, O God. I desire not to worry about frivolous things but to trust always and completely in you. Amen.

Week 9

Starting Over Again

Tremble, O earth, at the presence of the Lord, at the presence of the God of Jacob, who turns the rock into a pool of water, the flint into a spring of water. (Psalm 114:7-8)

The Desert Fathers have spoken about how the Word of God, like water, can soften the hard heart of a person. I think of their words and the words of the Psalmist as I work on the path this morning.

I have to go back to where the path began. A storm that hit the eastern United States blew down trees, scattered limbs, reeked havoc across this low-lying earth so that I must start over, from the beginning. It is almost as if there were never a path in these woods. Yet I know that because of the previous progress, it will be a little easier making a way than it was the first time.

This return to the starting place is a familiar theme in my spiritual journey. Time and time again a storm blows across my path. To cope, I fade back into unhealthy patterns and dysfunctional cycles.

It is a discouraging event to discover regression in one's life. Recognizing a repeated mistake, accepting that a lesson needs to be relearned is agonizingly painful. It is certainly disconcerting when I find I have not conquered some problem. But in the midst of the discontent I try to remember my limits, my humanness, without overwhelming myself with self-hatred or disappointment. To drown in guilt is of no consequence and only takes me further away from the path—the path that promises to lead me in the right direction.

19

I find that each time I must clean up after a storm and return to learn again, it comes a little easier. Like a stone-hard rock, I have been softened. I am more pliable. Perhaps, I remind myself, I will learn well enough so that the next time I will not have to begin again.

Meditation for Walking

What storms have blown across your path in recent weeks? In what unhealthy patterns or cycles do you continually find yourself? What is the hardest lesson you need to learn?

Prayer for Walking

God, let me put my trust in you so that when storms disrupt my way, I can always find the way to you. Amen.

Corners

*I rise before dawn and cry for help; I put my hope
in your words. My eyes are awake before each
watch of the night, that I may meditate on your
promise. (Psalm 119:147-148)*

i don't wear my Red Tennis Shoes anymore
somehow They just don't match my brown
or everyone else's brown.
It used not to matter
But that was when I wore Yellow
Very Bright Yellow
I certainly was smooth
Now I'm sharp.
four sharp corners
like everyone else.

I used to could roll and roll
(You can do that when You're round and smooth)
I would roll along with the Tree and the River
And I would roll on the Earth
And She would laugh
She liked it
Because She was round and smooth
And We matched
since i've gained my sharp corners
i can't roll.
the Earth cries when i try
my corners cut Her.
the Tree and the River call my name
and tell Me to come play
but i can't roll.

i can't run. i can't move.
like everyone else.

I don't think it will always be this way
I don't like not being able to move
I miss being round and smooth
and I like the Tree and the River
I like to hear the Earth laugh

but for now my corners are too sharp
and i'm too tired to try.
and now, now that i look around
me and everyone else
we match.

Meditation for Walking

Have you ever felt desperate to remember the promise of God? What in your life has become cornered?

Prayer for Walking

Smooth out the corners in my life. Hear my prayer, O Lord. Amen.

Week 11

Saints and Angels

Where can I go from your spirit? Or where can I flee from your presence? If I ascend to heaven, you are there; if I make my bed in Sheol, you are there. If I take the wings of the morning and settle at the farthest limits of the sea, even there your hand shall lead me, and your right hand shall hold me fast. If I say, "Surely the darkness shall cover me, and the light around me become night," even the darkness is not dark to you; the night is as bright as the day, for darkness is as light to you. (Psalm 139:7-12)

Therefore, since we are surrounded by so great a cloud of witnesses, let us also lay aside every weight and the sin that clings so closely, and let us run with perseverance the race that is set before us. (Hebrews 12:1)

"All night, all day, angels watching over me, my Lord. All day, all night, angels watching over me." I remember this song from my childhood. It is a loving and comforting song and memory. Like the psalm, it reminds me of God's pervading and loving presence as I walk this path.

When I was away on vacation earlier this week, my husband purchased several beautiful stone statues and lined my path with them. Most are angels. Some are kneeling, bent in prayer, one standing tall and firm, one lying on her belly, her head up and watching. There are saints also, for example, Francis of Assisi. He stands at the beginning, an invitation to experience the beauty of creation and the worshipfulness of all God's creatures. He serves to remind me to pay attention to simplicity in the ordering of creation and in the ordering of my life.

At the end of my path's way today is a saint whose name I do not know as of yet. He is a man, holding something in his arms I do not recognize. It appears to be a book. Perhaps as my path continues to wind down and around, I will meet some new saints and learn their story. For today it is enough to know I do not walk this path alone. Others have gone before me. Some will walk with me. Others will come later.

Saints and angels join us on our journeys. It is good to see and know their faces.

Meditation for Walking

Name some saints and angels who have been on or are now on your path. Think about what they have brought into your life.

Prayer for Walking

Thank you for the guidance that has come to me in the wisdom of saints and angels who walk along the path with me. May their lives be blessed in knowing that they have made my walk clearer and richer. Amen.

Week 12

Stumbling

A great company, they shall return here. With weeping they shall come, and with consolations I will lead them back, I will let them walk by brooks of water, in a straight path in which they shall not stumble. (Jeremiah 31:8b-9a)

I know all about stumbling. Literally, I understand because my path has many roots and uneven places. I am forever falling over unearthed stones and long unyielding roots. I also know this metaphorically when I consider all the things in my life that cause me to fall.

I stumble over my pride and my need to be right. I stumble over the desire to be recognized and honored and especially admired. I stumble over impatience and self-righteousness. It is a constant struggle of stumbles for me. I stand up only briefly and then find myself fallen on my face because once again, I have stumbled.

Just as I need to go back to the beginning again and again and walk the same path because I cannot seem to learn and unlearn and sustain the right way, over and over I stumble across stones I wished had been removed from my heart and spirit, stones that should have been removed ages ago.

I look forward to the day when my path is level and smooth; I will stumble no more. I look forward with great anticipation when I will see the rocks before they trip me and be able to miss their stony threat.

Until that day, however, the day of joy-weeping and soft feet, my homecoming day, I pray that God will grant me sufficient grace so that on the occasions I stumble, I will not fall upon someone else and also cause them to stumble.

Meditation for Walking

What causes you to stumble? What stones along your path can easily trip you?

Prayer for Walking

Rocks and stones that threaten to cause my downfall, I give to you, O God. May they soften and melt in the light of your love. Amen.

The Changing of Seasons

The grass withers, the flower fades, when the breath of the Lord blows upon it; surely the people are grass. The grass withers, the flower fades; but the word of our God will stand forever. (Isaiah 40:7-8)

Summer is ending. A new season fast approaches. The trees tell a story of departure as their leaves turn from the hearty depth of green to shades of autumn brilliance. The sun loses intensity; its light fades more quickly in the evening sky. Nature serves as a reminder that all things shall pass. All that lives must also die.

Just as my path winds into new territory and leaves behind what has become familiar and comfortable, so shall my faith move me into new areas of joy and discipline, and also sorrow and temptation.

There is grief in the passing of time. There is pain in moving from season to season. I begin to question what will survive. What will stand the passing of time? What does not wither and fade?

I find my answer in the book of Isaiah, from a prophet who welcomed and anticipated the passing of time. "But the word of our God will stand forever." God's word will not fade or wither or disappear into seasonal change. The word of God shall remain forever. God's word is a word of love and mercy, compassion and peace. No matter what changes occur in our lives, no matter what we must leave behind, or no matter to whom we must say goodbye, we can remain confident and sure in the unyielding word of God.

It is a statement of hope and comfort in the changing of seasons and the passing of time. We can stand in faith upon God's word. Let the seasons pass. Let time march. We are rooted, grounded, and sustained in a word that has no end.

Meditation for Walking

What has changed for you in recent months? To what or whom have you had to say goodbye? What have you seen fade and wither in your life, on your path? Find comfort in the ever-present word of God. Walk confidently in the Word, even as you live a life and walk a path laden with goodbyes.

Prayer for Walking

Order my steps in your Word, O Lord, that even as time passes swiftly, I shall not be lost. Amen.

Autumn

the middle passage

Week 14

Make Love Your Aim

Make love your aim; then be eager for the gifts of the Spirit. (1 Corinthians 14:1a RSV)

It is difficult to walk the path when I am angry. I can stomp. I can flail. But I find it impossible to walk. My heart and mind are filled with all kinds of negative energy and ideas that hinder me from the guiding principles of my faith, particularly that of love.

Let love be my aim; it has been my mantra this evening. In the midst of moving on my path I have tried to keep myself in the moment, bathing the person and the situation that have created such anger in me, in the light of God's love. I have tried to maintain a steady breath, breathing in compassion and mercy and breathing out resentment and bitterness. I am trying to get back on the path of love.

Being mad with someone is like overlooking a stone along the journey. It embeds itself deeper and deeper into the walkway. The stone eventually becomes a part of the path, making it a way that is no longer smooth and straight. The edges of the stone are barely visible; but it's there, a place upon which to stumble, a trying moment with a rake or hoe. And the longer it remains in the path, the more difficult it is to have it removed.

I pray that I might have the insight to see those stones, recognize them for what they are, and permit them to be released from the path, from my spirit. I understand that such stones can only be pulled up with forgiveness and love, which can only come about through prayer and communication. I pray that these rocks, these hardened places of anger and bitterness, can be used as markers along the edges of my path to remind me of the great power anger

31

can possess and the great spaces that can be created when they are removed.

It is only when the stones of anger are taken away that the gifts of the Spirit can flow freely along the path. When the stones are gone, there are spaces that are open for God's love and grace.

Meditation for Walking

What has caused you to be angry recently? Envision those situations or persons as being brought into the circle of God's love.

Prayer for Walking

Remove the stones, God, that block the way of love in my life. Help me in my walk to make love my aim. Amen.

Week 15

Sharing Your Path

Do not neglect to show hospitality to strangers, for by doing that some have entertained angels without knowing it. (Hebrews 13:2)

At the forks in your road you encounter other lives. Getting to know them or not, merging with them or passing them by, depends solely on the choice you make in a moment; though you may not know it, your whole life and the lives of those close to you are at stake when you choose whether to go straight or turn aside.

—Susanne Tamaro
Follow Your Heart

Choosing to let someone walk the path with me is sometimes made in a moment and sometimes it is made over great passages of time. Sometimes such choices are not even made by me at all. Perhaps I do not even want the presence of this one or that; but they must share a bit of the walk with me if I am going to learn what it is I must learn.

Those with whom I walk briefly teach me great wisdom. Like a shooting star, the lesson begins and ends with great clarity. It happens so quickly, I am often amazed I was even paying attention. And I suppose there are times when I am not.

Then there are those who take many steps with me, a husband, a best friend, a spiritual guide, a sister. There are those who enter my life with a mutual choice of companionship. I savor our journeys together. From them I learn loyalty, patience, love—lessons that take a lifetime to cultivate and nurture.

In reflecting upon the relationships, both those I enjoy and even those I don't so much enjoy, I begin to realize that I am blessed by all the people who share my path. I am blessed by the paths they walk, blessed by the intimacy we share, and even when they are gone, by the memories we have created.

Our paths, though our own, are also intended to be shared with others. For what does it profit a person to speak in tongues or have the gift of prophecy or have faith so as to remove mountains or give all that is possessed to the poor or even turn over one's body to be sacrificed—if there is no relationship, no love? And love cannot be grown in isolation. It can only widen and deepen when it is given away and thereby returned.

Meditation for Walking

Who walks your path with you? Whom have you encountered most recently? How have they blessed your journey?

Prayer for Walking

Thank you, God, for those who walk my path with me. Open my heart to what I need to learn from them. Amen.

Learning Balance

Finally, beloved, whatever is true, whatever is honorable, whatever is just, whatever is pure, whatever is pleasing, whatever is commendable, if there is any excellence and if there is anything worthy of praise, think about these things. (Philippians 4:8)

For everything there is a season, and a time for every matter under heaven. (Ecclesiastes 3:1)

I am discouraged today. It seems I have not gotten very far with the path. I look out over the forest: the vines, the trees, the limbs and stumps, the uneven ground, the stones. I feel like maybe this was a silly undertaking after all. It appears futile. I have so far to go.

Oh, I know all the right answers. I know Paul's words to the church at Philippi by heart: "Think about these [good] things." Do not dwell on that which is discouraging or overwhelming. Do not focus on the obstacles; focus on the path. Do not watch for the progress, but rather pay attention to the process. Do not become engrossed in what lies ahead; but instead stay in the moment, in this day. And yet, at times, I am caught up in the temptation to quit, to give up, to go back.

Of course, the lesson from Ecclesiastes reminds us there are, in fact, times to keep and times to throw away. There are times when we are meant to let go, to kill, to break down, to tear, and to hate. But there are also times when we are to hang on, not give up, to seek and love and fight.

I have discovered that much of my learning comes in finding the balance of when to keep and when not to keep, when to press forward and when to back off. Having such a balance is a secret, I am convinced, to joyful living.

I know I cannot quit this path. It indeed has a beginning, and it will have an ending; but it is not here. Not yet. Not now. I only need to remind myself that pace is not the ultimate measure. Results cannot be exacted in yards and feet, for many strides are made when we simply stick to the way we have started. Today, I journey on, trying not to be overwhelmed with what lies ahead or discouraged by what has not been completed.

Meditation for Walking

What discourages you? In what aspect of your life do you feel overwhelmed or frustrated? Are you able to give these aspects of your life to God?

Prayer for Walking

Create in me, O God, an encouraged and faithful heart. Amen.

Week 17

Milestones

But those who wait for the Lord shall renew their strength, they shall mount up with wings like eagles, they shall run and not be weary, they shall walk and not faint. (Isaiah 40:31)

O Gracious God, it was a long journey for me to get here. Yet I'm not tired, because you've strengthened me. It was a tough journey. Yet I didn't give up, because you've comforted me. In front of me I see a narrow and rough road through which no one has yet walked. But I'm not afraid, because you are alive. Help me always to be faithful to you and to your people for whom I was called. Lead me to wherever you want me to be. Strengthen me to live what I believe.

—Kyung-Lim-Shin-Lee
"Strength for Difficult Passages"

This ordination prayer taken from *Wellsprings* journal reminds me of my own ordination. It was a significant event in my life, a milestone. And I remember feeling thrilled that finally I had made it to that *place*, that crossroads in my path. Looking back now, I'm mindful of how far I had to go from there, how far I have to go from here. The service of ordination, however, was a milestone, a marker of strength and assurance and support. It remains a powerful memory that serves to buoy me up when I'm feeling a little weak, unassured, unsupported.

It is important to have such milestones for ourselves along our paths. There is a need for places, markers where we can look back and remember significant renderings of

God's blessings and the support of some teacher, mentor, or community. The highlights are necessary for the journey to continue—not just at the time of their happenings, but also in times much later. Recognizing the importance of such milestones reminds me of a character in a movie who collected stones for all of the important events and memories in his life. At the time of his death there was a pocketful of stones, symbolic of a heart full of memories.

As I walk this literal path, I find myself being drawn to collecting the stones I unearth. I don't put them in my pockets, but I do gather them together and place them near the feet of the angels or at certain corners, bends of the path. They serve to remind me that milestones, rituals, and relationships need to be marked, honored, and remembered. These will be the stones that remind me at another section of the path that I have been loved, valued, and blessed. The stones become tangible symbols for the memories I have encountered along the path.

Meditation for Walking

What are the significant markers on your path? What have been your milestones?

Prayer for Walking

Thank you, God, for those places and people and events that mark growth and progress while I walk along this journey. Amen.

The Promise of God

The days are surely coming, says the Lord, when I will make a new covenant with the house of Israel and the house of Judah. It will not be like the covenant that I made with their ancestors when I took them by the hand to bring them out of the land of Egypt—a covenant that they broke, though I was their husband, says the Lord. But this is the covenant that I will make with the house of Israel after those days, says the Lord: I will put my law within them, and I will write it on their hearts; and I will be their God, and they shall be my people. (Jeremiah 31:31-33)

I am thinking about promises, God's in particular. Many times I get confused about God's promises. The promise is not that we shall uncover or follow a path and experience no pain or stumbling blocks or disappointments. The promise is not that we shall go in the direction we had planned in the beginning, that evil might not draw us from the destination we had hoped to meet. God's promises are not always the agenda we set and look to keep when we are trying to put meat on the bones of a vision.

In moving along my path I realize the journey hasn't always gone where I wanted it to go. Sometimes I have had to take a longer way across treacherous terrain, and sometimes I've gone a shorter way and missed what I thought I should have experienced. God's promises are not always about safety or fun. And unfortunately, they are not usually about pleasantries as much as we might like them to be. These are the promises we carve for ourselves out of wishes.

Beneath and beyond all the visions and agendas and wishes we build is the promise of God: "I will be your God, and you shall be my people." It is a promise that over and over again reminds us that nothing shall separate us from that relationship, that love. It is a promise regarding the ultimate safety of our spirit, a safety that speaks not about harm of the body or destruction of possessions or worldly attachments, but a safety that reminds us that when we are through falling, we land right in the arms of God.

The ideas we conjure up about God's ultimate promise may come true, or they may not. But regardless of those minor fulfillments or nonfulfillments, God will still be there, as present as the promise that God's name is written on our hearts.

Meditation for Walking

Do you ever get confused about what God has promised? How do you handle disappointments, your path going in a different direction than originally hoped? Are you able to find strength in the knowledge of God's ultimate promise, that God's name is written on your heart?

Prayer for Walking

Keep my eyes on you, God of love, wherever my path may take me. Amen.

Carry Me, Lord

Therefore lift your drooping hands and strengthen your weak knees, and make straight paths for your feet, so that what is lame may not be put out of joint, but rather be healed. (Hebrews 12:12-13)

And when the rain falls
And when sorrow calls
Carry me, Lord, carry me.

When I am blind to your peace
Can find no sweet release
Carry me, Lord, carry me.

Pick up my tired and drooping arms
Shelter me from all that harms
Fill up those barren places
And color the empty spaces
O My Lord, carry me.

From valley to mountain
From desert to fountain
I pray, I say, I shout all this day,
Carry me, Lord, carry me.

Meditation for Walking

How do you pray when your arms are drooping?
Where is God for you when you're weak and tired?

Prayer for Walking

Be my strength, O God. Lift my eyes to you. Amen.

Week 20

Walking in the Presence of God

For you have delivered my soul from death, and my feet from falling, so that I may walk before God in the light of life. (Psalm 56:13)

Walking in the presence of God. The psalmist does not write about destination, pie-in-the-sky-when-we-die jargon. The psalmist writes about walking in the presence of God.

Recently I visited my dear friend, Anna. She and her husband are the proud parents of thirteen-month-old Evan. Evan is just learning to walk without the support of furniture or walls; he is beginning to walk completely on his own. But because the young toddler learned to walk by holding the hand of his mom or his dad, he now walks with one arm held high in the air while he uses the other to touch or grasp whatever interests him.

It is a curious sight. Yet, if you watch Evan long enough, you almost believe he's really holding hands with someone taller, sturdier than he, someone you just can't see. You almost begin to believe he is not walking alone.

Evan's walk served to remind me of what it means to "walk before God." It is to walk with one arm up, straight in the air, acknowledging that we need God's support, God's hand to guide us and hold us up.

God walks with us whether we keep our hands up or not. But wouldn't life be richer, fuller, deeper, and wiser if we acknowledged and called upon God more frequently? Wouldn't our paths seem more complete if we called attention to the one who walks beside us? And even if those who walk near us think it looks strange or odd that we walk in a different posture, wouldn't our lives be more

43

clearly walks of abundant life if we looked like we were walking in the presence of God?

There is room on the journey for both ourselves and God. It took the experience of a new path walker, a child, to demonstrate this for me.

Meditation for Walking

Where along your path is it most difficult to believe that you are in the presence of God? Are you able to visualize God being with you when you walk this part of your journey?

Prayer for Walking

God who walks with me, let me find you in every step I take. Amen.

𝒯𝒶𝓀𝒾𝓃ℊ 𝓡𝑒𝓈𝓉

Come to me, all you that are weary and are carrying heavy burdens, and I will give you rest. Take my yoke upon you, and learn from me; for I am gentle and humble in heart, and you will find rest for your souls. For my yoke is easy, and my burden is light. (Matthew 11:28-30)

Yesterday I pushed the path around a tree making a sharp corner to the left, and then I stopped for the day. When I returned to work, I looked ahead about ten feet and noticed a natural clearing beyond my ending place. (It's somewhat silly to me how I claim to be "pushing" the path when it's clear the path is pushing me! It is as if the path is already present—I am simply digging beneath the pine straw, the vines, and rotten logs to find it.)

The natural clearing speaks as a resting place would speak. "Clear it all out. Bring logs on which to sit. Here is a place to focus. Here is a natural resting place on this path."

I too often forget that "resting" is an integral part of the path. Feeling as if I am required to blaze across the earth in some missionary zeal, I overlook the fact that even God rested as part of the creation path. (Of course, God was finished!)

There must be places where I stop to reflect on where I have been, where I am, and where I am going. There must be Sabbaths—not just once in awhile when I'm exhausted, but regular times to sit still, not plan or worry or talk. There must be time to sit in the silence, or as it is in these woods where I walk and make my path, sit in the great cacophony of forest and village noises. There are children at a neighboring school enjoying recess. Dairy cows are behind us. I hear chain saws and tractors clearing other paths.

If I didn't stop and take the rest that is necessary for uncovering and following a spiritual path, I would not enjoy the progress, the lack of progress, or the adventure of it all.

As a reminder of the need to wear a gentle yoke, a new creature has made himself known. He's quite a scary critter, looking part snake, part lizard. I guess he is a salamander. At least a foot long, he had been resting, perhaps beginning a sort of seasonal hibernation. He was as surprised to see me as I him; but he, being in the state of rest, did not move very quickly. In fact, he barely moved at all. I worked around him, quite sure my path is not meant to overpower his.

A visitor, I came across him—or he came across me. He is a slow and gentle reminder to rest, to take Sabbath. It, too, is part of the path.

Meditation for Walking

How do you honor "Sabbath" in your life? What do you do or undo to make sure rest is a part of your journey?

Prayer for Walking

Teach me the need to rest today. Amen.

Abandoned Love

But I have this against you, that you have abandoned the love you had at first. (Revelation 2:4)

Ah, love that torments me
out of contentment and ease of living,
stretch yourself across my weakened eyes
and cast the colors of your light
into my vision
That I may see as you see.

Ah, peace that melts the hardened edges
of my battered, sin-filled heart,
mold yourself about my leaking spirit
and shore up the corners of the storms
that blow into my thinking
That I may dance as you dance.

Ah, joy that sparks fire
into damp, dark caves of flesh,
burn hard and deep until
the sorrow is seared
and I can remember the breeze of freedom.

Ah, Spirit that once ignited me,
rekindle that which has died out.
Awake and renew and remind,
for it seems I have forgotten.
I have dismissed.
I have abandoned.

Meditation for Walking

Have you abandoned what you had in the beginning of your path? How can you rekindle that which has died down?

Prayer for Walking

Forgive me, O God, when I forget the love with which I began. Amen.

Bare Feet

Keep your feet from going unshod and your throat from thirst. (Jeremiah 2:25a)

Keeping one's feet from going unshod is to pay attention not to let them become uncovered, bare. The path is not a race, though sometimes I feel the urge to go further, dig deeper. The temptation for me is to hurry through the day's work, literally running out of my shoes, while trying to make great progress.

In the last few months, however, I have learned that if I try to do too much too quickly, I miss the splendor of God's goodness in the small things—creatures around me who seek, in their own ways, to worship. There are the delicate threads of a spider web just above my head, a slight angle of sunlight, the drop of rain balanced on a leaf. All of creation speaks to the glory of God.

I've also learned that if I move too quickly, I risk damage not just to my spirit but also to my body. Carelessness breeds disaster. When I do not pay attention to the design and nature of the vines around me, I easily become a victim to poison ivy. If I try to do too much clearing and raking, I am easily reminded in very sore muscles and particularly in the wounded/healed/wounded places in my body, especially my neck.

Pace must be monitored. Product is not the thing to be valued. Process is the open door through which I walk to discover. I learn from what I experience, not from what I use merely to show to others what I have completed.

Process and reflection and encounter, these are the great teachers. To learn from them, I must walk slowly and carefully. If I am zooming through and over my path, I am likely to miss all three, only to arrive at the end having observed and learned nothing. If I am to know the great lessons of life, I must be willing to pay attention to learn them.

Meditation for Walking

Are your feet bare? What are the little things you notice on your walk today?

Prayer for Walking

Help me to slow down, O God, that I may notice your surprises of grace along my path. Amen.

Angels Bearing Gifts

Then he lay down under the broom tree and fell asleep. Suddenly an angel touched him and said to him, "Get up and eat." He looked, and there at his head was a cake baked on hot stones, and a jar of water. He ate and drank, and lay down again. (1 Kings 19:5-6)

I love the story of the prophet Elijah. Not long after he enjoyed great success at Mount Carmel where he and God defeated Baal and his prophets, Elijah ran scared, head long into the wilderness. He was afraid because Queen Jezebel, angry at this prophetic showdown, herself being a worshiper of Baal, threatened the prophet's life and sent Elijah running.

I love that God comes in the form and shape of an angel who nurtures and feeds Elijah. There is no chastising, no anger at Elijah for his lack of faith. Only rest and cake and water are brought to him. And then there is more rest and cake and water. And when Elijah is fed and rested, he is able to continue on his journey and also to hear God's message that comes not in an earthquake or great wind or fire but rather in a still, small voice.

I have been blessed in my life with many angels, usually, though not always, in the form of a woman. She brings to me cakes and pies and jams. Sometimes the angel, in the form of a man, brings me juice and crackers while I busy myself at the typewriter or phone. These angels remind me that I am a physical being and that I must, therefore, have food and rest, nutrients and refreshment.

It is easy along our life's path to move from mountaintop to wilderness unaware of our bodies' needs until we are broken, sick, or malnourished. It is important to take time for rest. It is essential, especially in times of grief and sorrow, to eat healthy, to give our bodies proper sustenance.

The prophet Elijah was met by God in his greatest need. God came to God's servant and bid him eat and rest. Only after his physical needs were met did God speak to him God's will. And only after his physical needs were met was Elijah able to hear God's instructions for the next part of the path.

If you find yourself in a wilderness hungry for some message from God, needing some direction, pay attention to what your body requires. Only after you are fed and rested can God's voice and will become clear.

Meditation for Walking

Who are the angels who have nurtured and cared for you? How does God come to you in your hour of greatest need?

Prayer for Walking

When I run scared, O God, help me find my rest in you. Amen.

Walking by Faith

For we walk by faith, not by sight. (2 Corinthians 5:7)

As I walk along this path, it is easier and seemingly more practical to watch where I am going instead of trusting the direction of the path or the Creator of both me and the forest where the path is located.

Today, as I reflect on my work, I feel the need to build or add another stretch of a path to symbolize the issue of choice. One path will go directly through a spot of woods, while another will go up and around a few trees and then down to meet the other way, merging back into the original path.

By allowing for such a split and merge, I am suddenly aware of how many decisions we must make in a day, a week, a life span. Most of the time we are desperate for some outcome, to know by sight, that we are making the right decision. Yet it is rare when we are given such insight. We must remember that we are walking by faith.

Sometimes my choices feel so ultimate. I worry and grieve. I stay afraid that I will make the wrong choice. But in the activity and reflection of today I am comforted in the realization that not all choices are so monumental. There is room and latitude for more than one right choice. There are decisions to be made that bear significant conse-quences, all important decisions that should receive a lot of attention. But there are also decisions that lend themselves to a "no-lose" outcome.

If I choose to walk up and around the trees, I may be going a bit out of the way; I may not get to the merge as quickly as if I walked straight through. But this path, the spiritual path, is not about speed or pace. This path is about the journey itself.

It is okay that I needed a little extra time, an extra twist and turn. I need not be so hard on myself if it appears the choice I made took me the long way around. Perhaps the long way is the way I most needed to walk on this day, and I can trust that I will come to the place I need to be. After all, this is a path about faith and not about sight.

Meditation for Walking

What decisions have you made that you felt took you the long way around? Can you find any benefit in the extra time it took?

Prayer for Walking

Grant me the knowledge of your will in every choice I make, dear God, and no matter the outcome, let me abide in you. Amen.

Week 26

Be still, and know that I am God! (Psalm 46:10a)

I feel the approach of winter. Everything seems to slow down as we wait for the season of stillness.

Introspection and stillness are not states of being most people in our culture value. We are praised for fast thinking, fast talking, and quick action. Though most everyone knows the story of the tortoise and the rabbit and remembers that the tortoise, in a slow and plotting manner, beat the rabbit at the end of the race, we still tend to seek and value a quick-paced life that makes no space or time for a season of winter or an hour of stillness.

Being quiet or still is seen as a weakness in the business world. Silence is often viewed as a liability, a measure of incompetence. We have adapted this value in our spiritual and emotional lives. We have become so action-oriented that we see stillness and nonaction as unnecessary and useless. But the Psalmist reminds us we need the season of winter in our lives. We need the opportunity to be quiet, still. We learn in the season of stillness that we shall experience the knowledge of God.

A friend once taught me a meditation based on this Scripture verse. You begin by saying the entire sentence, You say this three to five times, slowly and with deep breaths. Then you begin leaving off a word and repeating the new shorter sentence in the same way, slowly and with deep breaths.

> Be still and know that I am God.
> Be still and know that I am.
> Be still and know.
> Be still.
> Be.

It is a beautiful way to center oneself and calm down. It is an excellent way to bring a sense of winter and stillness in our crazy lives.

Meditation for Walking

"Be still, and know that I am God!" Perhaps it is only in our stillness that we can know for sure.

Use the meditation exercise as mentioned above. Take the opportunity to implement it as a part of every day.

Prayer for Walking

Help me, O God, to be still and know. Amen.

Winter

deep into the woods

Waiting

*As for me, this is my covenant with you: You shall
be the ancestor of a multitude of nations. No
longer shall your name be Abram, but your name
shall be Abraham; for I have made you the ancestor of a multitude of nations. (Genesis 17:4-5)*

Abraham had been given the promise a great deal of time
before God spoke these words. He was still waiting for this
old promise to be fulfilled.

There is much in the gospel story about waiting. There
is almost as much, it seems, about waiting as there is about
"getting there," or finding the long-awaited answer. I think
specifically of Advent—the wait for the Messiah, the anticipation of the arrival, the preparation for the event.

I'm not very good at waiting. It has rained all week, so
I've been unable to work on the path. Finally there comes
a day with sunshine and time and space to work, but I have
hurt my back; so now I'll have to wait some more. In the
meantime the forest seems to stretch for miles, and the
path's progress is just cutting into its edge.

It is easy to get discouraged, to say words like, "I give
up; it just isn't going to happen." But then I remember sto-
ries such as Abraham and Sarah waiting for a child, Noah in
the ark waiting for sunshine, Mary and Martha waiting for
Jesus after the death of their brother Lazarus, Jesus in the
tomb for three days, descending, ascending, waiting to face
his followers.

There is an element of the promise and its purpose that
is actualized within the practice of waiting. It is not a passive, indifferent act; rather, it is a living into the promise, an
anticipation that the experience of looking forward to the

coming event is as rich and important as the hour of fulfillment.

Isn't it true that as we journey on our path, working towards some goal, once the goal is reached—the promise fulfilled—we realize that part of the fulfillment, part of the joy happened in the time of waiting?

Meditation for Walking

How do you handle waiting? For what are you waiting now? How can you practice peace in the midst of unfulfilled promises?

Prayer for Walking

God of promises, let me find peace in my time of waiting. Amen.

Tiny Steps

As a deer longs for flowing streams, so my soul longs for you, O God. My soul thirsts for God, for the living God. When shall I come and behold the face of God? My tears have been my food day and night, while people say to me continually, "Where is your God?" These things I remember, as I pour out my soul: how I went with the throng, and led them in procession to the house of God, with glad shouts and songs of thanksgiving, a multitude keeping festival. Why are you cast down, O my soul, and why are you disquieted within me? Hope in God; for I shall again praise him, my help. (Psalm 42:1-5)

I didn't get very far today on the path. The way seemed rougher somehow. I kept looking around thinking, "These are the same woods. I'm using the same tools. I have the same strength as I did before! Why does it seem to be so much more difficult to push aside the straw and sticks and debris? Why is it taking so long?"

My friend died on Saturday, Ronnie, the young man whose wedding I was planning on the second day of unbuilding the path. In a year's time I had baptized, married, and buried him. It all seemed too much in too short of time. I realize that as his pastor and friend, I need to grieve. I have the right to be angry and say he was too young. I can even say I hate this job that requires me to say words in a service of worship that ring empty, make promises that seem impossible.

I need to be spoken to, comforted, held. I had hoped this funeral would not have been so difficult, that it would not have cost me so much emotionally. I had planned on "getting a little further" in my work as a pastor.

Peggy, Ronnie's wife, asked me how she would be able to go on without the love and presence of her husband. I think I said something like, "You just do it; you get up in the morning, you wash your face, you breathe, and you look to take only very small steps."

I am learning that it is often the same way on my spiritual journey. I move only a little at a time. They are baby steps in comparison to where I think I need to go. But in the face of death and sadness and loss, it is the pace I am required to take. I move; and slowly, over a lengthy period of time, I discover that I've made it to a new place.

Today my steps are tiny. May God have mercy on my soul.

Meditation for Walking

What loss have you suffered recently? How do you handle grief?

Prayer for Walking

As I take both big and tiny steps, let me feel your presence with me. Amen.

The Life That Christ Lives in Me

I have been crucified with Christ; and it is no longer I who live, but it is Christ who lives in me. (Galatians 2:19b-20a)

Sometimes I can't help but realize I keep trying to take over the path myself. I am sure it is I who knows a better way; it is I who can keep forging the journey ahead. I frequently discover that it is my life, my desires, my needs that rule the path instead of Christ's life living in me. I forget the relationship I am to have with Christ. I forget that my desires and needs are to become one with his since it is no longer I who live but Christ who lives in me.

I am often drawn back to the essence of this verse in Galatians when I have to go back to the beginning and start again. I find myself once again going over the path from the start to where I last finished, seeing again the places I have already seen, areas I have already worked, problems I thought were solved and completed, issues I had presumed were dead and buried.

It is a frustrating process, having to begin again, having to go back over things I thought I had learned, areas of the way I thought were clean. Sticks and straw once again clutter the center of the path. And so using a yard rake with its long, slender, bending fingers, I start over.

It is not as difficult to move across this portion of the path as it was the first time I came through. The earth is loose, the path more clearly marked. But it still is disconcerting to need to begin again, to walk from the starting place again. It is humbling but very important to understand that I am unable to forge ahead until I've gone back to the beginning, making sure I've learned what I needed to learn, cleared away what needs to be cleared away.

When I forget who directs my path, who has set me upon this path, I am quickly lost and run down by the forest that surrounds me. There are necessary occasions when I must begin again to remember whose life I live, whose path I walk.

Meditation for Walking

What parts of your life do you try to control? Let these be the parts of your path you give to God today.

Prayer for Walking

Christ Jesus, live in me so that I might live in you. Amen.

The Source of All

*Who will separate us from the love of Christ? Will
hardship, or distress, or persecution, or famine, or
nakedness, or peril, or sword? . . . No, in all these
things we are more than conquerors through him
who loved us. For I am convinced that neither
death, nor life, nor angels, nor rulers, nor things
present, nor things to come, nor powers, nor
height, nor depth, nor anything else in all creation, will be able to separate us from the love of
God in Christ Jesus our Lord. (Romans 8:35, 37-
39)*

"There must be a way to know the future," the tree said.

"No," the rock replied. "The water passes through; and
bit by bit I feel myself changed. I know I will not be the
same tomorrow as I am today. Not ever again will I look
and feel exactly this way. But I have no way of knowing
who I will be."

"No idea?" The little tree pulled her limbs close to
herself and sighed.

"Oh, there's some idea. A notion. A shelf to rest my
hopes on. For I believe in the kindness of the water, the
innocence in the way it dances, the joy in its rhythm. It
would not harm me, not intentionally."

"Yes, but see," the little tree rustled her leaves, standing
high and tall. "That's the thing. It may not hurt you with
intention, but you can still be damaged by its ceaseless
motion! You can still be hurt!" She bent and touched the
broken place on her trunk.

"Ah, but here is another thing." The rock steadied herself in the stream. The water rushed across her. "Even

greater than my faith in the water is my faith in the source of the water. For even better than having no intention for harm is its intention for good. And though there are many others to consider, this is the greatest thing."

And with that, the little rock rolled on ahead.

***

The idea of this story came to me as I walked along a path during a recent retreat. I like the notion of a conversation between a tree and a stone. I like more, however, the idea of the goodness of the source of all. Perhaps the stream and her stones, like the forest, can teach me.

Meditation for Walking

In considering the source of all beings, what is the greatest thing for you?

Prayer for Walking

Help me to let go like the rock in this story, trusting that the love of God will not take me anywhere the grace of God will not be. Amen.

Having Not Yet Reached Perfection

> *It is not that I have already achieved this. I have
> not yet reached perfection, but I press on, hoping
> to take hold of that for which Christ once took
> hold of me. I press towards the finishing line, to
> win the heavenly prize to which God has called
> me in Christ Jesus. (Philippians 3:12-14 RSV)*

Perfection seems to be such a lofty goal for one who is so imperfect. Surely that is not my task. At first glance I wonder if Paul was having one of his off days when he wrote this passage. I understand the concept of pressing towards the finish line. I embrace the idea of "hoping to take hold of that which Christ once took hold of me." But perfection?

Perhaps it is my interpretation of perfection that is skewed. Maybe I am placing human form upon a divine notion. Would my idea of perfection look the same as the "perfect" idea of God? My view of perfection has to do with order, clarity, step-by-step motion with no visible flaw. I think of being perfect as meaning coloring only within the lines, pushing no boundaries, staying stringent and clean.

Possibly the godly view of perfection is sometimes this way, but mostly it is something totally different. Can a sunset be perfect? Is a rainbow perfect? Was the act of creation perfect? It is, I know, difficult to know from this late date of human destruction. Ozone layers and rain forests surely cannot be judged from this time in history. Yet even at God's whim of designing a world, were all things meant to be perfect? And what about the storms of nature, the spontaneous volcanic eruption or quake of earth? Are not these violent and imperfect elements of nature also of the original design?

Perhaps I am looking through a dim and broken lens. My vision of perfection is forced and unclear. Perhaps the matter of perfection is not about order or clarity or even having no visible flaws. Perhaps instead it is about casting off any layer of judgment or comparative analysis and more about opening to all that is around me. It is setting no limits to the possibilities that lie within my heart, bringing forth the brilliance and weaknesses that dance side by side within me.

I do not believe complete order and clarity are the divine interpretation of perfection. It must not be so. For indeed, if such a judgment was set in place, there would have been no room for the cross or the empty grave. The death and resurrection were as messy and chaotic and jumbled as any events in history. Yet when has the world known such a grace as this to perfect what lies at the heart of brokenness and imperfection?

Pressing on towards perfection involves putting aside the glasses the world has put before our eyes, dismissing the human table of measuring and scoring. Leaning towards perfection is letting go of perfectionist notions and accepting an entirely new perception. Leaning towards perfection is the recognition of the divine in every living being, flawed and otherwise.

Meditation for Walking

How does being a perfectionist cause trouble in your life?

Prayer for Walking

Let me see the world, O Risen Christ, through the eyes of the one who saved it. Amen.

Trees Clapping Their Hands

*For you shall go out in joy, and be led back in
peace; the mountains and the hills before you
shall burst into song, and all the trees of the field
shall clap their hands. Instead of the thorn shall
come up the cypress; instead of the brier shall
come up the myrtle; and it shall be to the Lord for
a memorial, for an everlasting sign that shall not
be cut off. (Isaiah 55:12-13)*

Trees clapping their hands, what an unusual notion! Trees
don't even have hands. Arms, maybe—great, long, leafy
arms—but what are the hands of a tree?

The prophet Isaiah was reaching with great anticipation for metaphors to describe the return home for the
exiles. Imagine the thought of going home after so many
years being forced away. Imagine reaching the city gates
and knowing you will not have to leave again. Imagine the
joy, the unspeakable joy, in going back to your land, your
place of birth, the resting/burial ground of your family.
Imagine the shock of pleasure in knowing you are finally
safe, finally out of harm's way, finally home.

Thinking of mountains and hills breaking into cries of
joy and all the trees in the countryside suddenly bearing
hands to clap doesn't seem so far-fetched.

Haven't we all longed for something/someone to go
back to? Haven't we all ached for something so deeply,
grieved for something so desperately that to think of the
return to that lost place or person or time is to think what
is up will come down, what is rooted and bound shall be
set free, and what is orderly and natural will suddenly
become joyously chaotic and unnaturally amazing? Isn't it

true that when we mourn the loss of the treasures of our hearts, we know that if the loss were restored, nothing would ever be the same again?

As I stand among these trees, these tall beautiful pine trees that grow in the place of camel-thorns, I am quieted by the rush of wind through their dancing needles. I think of joy long gone, friends who are away, the death of dreams, the angry words that still separate me from another. Suddenly, a fleeting thought reminds me there shall be a time and place when these things and relationships shall be restored, a time and place when all of God's children will go out in joy, in abounding peace. And as the thought circles round about my head, opening my ears to impossibilities becoming possible, I think I hear the faint sound of wood striking wood. A low but undeniable response, the forest thunders with applause.

Meditation for Walking

How would you describe unspeakable joy? What are the images or metaphors you would use? What has been lost in your life that you hope will one day be restored?

Prayer for Walking

God, who leads us in joy and peace, walk with me today so that I may believe in a hopeful reunion when I shall see you and all that has been lost, face to face. Amen.

The Tongue Is a Fire

*The tongue is a fire. The tongue is placed among
our members as a world of iniquity; it stains the
whole body, sets on fire the cycle of nature, and is
itself set on fire by hell. (James 3:6)*

Ouch! The author of James doesn't soften the blow one bit!
Rather, the reader is given a harsh note about the mushy,
pink mouth appendage that seems so harmless, compared
to the tight fist or the kicking foot.

It seems, however, that I have seen more violence done
by that harmless muscle than by fists or teeth or feet. The
words we use against one another, the gossip we spread,
the lies we let fall from our lips produce much damage.
Much evil could be stopped if we would just shut our
mouths and hold our tongues.

It is silent in the woods today. Winter has deadened the
ground, quieted the busy life. Most of the animals that are
so active in the other seasons have grown still, asleep. It is
in this time, this holding of nature's tongue, that I am
reminded of my need for silence. I am reminded of the
need for seasons in my life, spaces in services of worship,
minutes or even hours in the day when I keep silence.
Perhaps if I bridled my tongue for just a little bit, I might
quiet the evil that comes so easily when I talk without
thought.

Surely in our spiritual lives, the paths we walk, we must
have some space carved out, set aside, for silence. If not, we
will most certainly miss the messages in the wind, the sighs
and signs of a thickening winter, the gold of silence.
Dietrich Bonhoeffer wrote in *Life Together*:

Silence is nothing else but waiting for God's Word and coming from God's Word with a blessing. But everybody knows that this is something that needs to be practiced and learned, in these days when talkativeness prevails. Real silence, real stillness, really holding one's tongue comes only as the sober consequence of spiritual stillness.

Ecclesiastes 3:7 reminds us there is "a time to keep silence and a time to speak." As we walk along our paths we must on occasion hold our tongues, keep silence, and listen for the word of God. It is the only way to proceed.

Meditation for Walking

How are you at keeping silence? Can you add a time of silence in your walk today?

Prayer for Walking

Teach me, O God, to learn self-control, especially when it comes to excessive talking. Amen.

Do Not Lose Heart

*So we do not lose heart. Even though our outer
nature is wasting away, our inner nature is being
renewed day by day. For this slight momentary
affliction is preparing us for an eternal weight of
glory beyond all measure, because we look not at
what can be seen but at what cannot be seen; for
what can be seen is temporary, but what cannot
be seen is eternal. (2 Corinthians 4:16-18)*

We returned home today to find some trees cut down that
stood dangerously near our house. The beginning 25 or 30
feet of my path is destroyed. Near the path I've been clearing another large and forced way has been made by the
dragging of trees. It goes straight down into the heart of
the forest, creating an opening that seems to overshadow
the narrow twisting path that is mine.

There really is no way to describe the sight. It is ugly.
The land is scarred. Rocks are strewn. The borders have
disappeared. The tiny sapling so carefully preserved in the
beginning of this journey is ravaged and broken.

I did not want the trees removed. I rarely do well with
ideas of realism or rationalism, so when I was told of the
danger of storms in winter and spring and the endless possibilities of our possessions being destroyed, I still saw no
reason to tear down the trees.

I now understand the significance of loss. I struggle
with severe disillusionment, the dream suddenly snatched
away. And from there it's only a very small step to self-
debasement. "It was a stupid idea anyway. What good
would this dumb little path do?" Then I face the difficult
lesson of detachment to possessions, including personal

accomplishment. There is the undying truth that beats in my brain: one must not be attached, not even to the path itself, only to the maker of the path. For even though one may worship what appears to be a godly idea (church, a saint, the Bible, a path), it is still not God. It has become an idol and must be given over.

Tonight in my time of prayer (nothing more than choking tears and groans of despair) I sat up to read some Scripture. I was given the passage from Paul's letter to the church at Corinth. It spoke of "this slight momentary affliction." I find the guidance to fix my eyes on the things that are unseen, not on the things that are seen.

My path is cut into a woods that on paper may be my woods, but I do not possess them. For really, who can own a tree? How does one make a stream or mountain his alone? And this path, this gift of a journey is not about the things seen, not about the progress or distance or appearance, but rather about the things unseen, the journey of the spirit. It is a powerful but painful lesson that comes from troubles. For only at the onset of trouble are we really forced to face where our eyes have been fixed.

Meditation for Walking

What were the circumstances of your last major disappointment? Based on the situation, where would you say your eyes were fixed?

Prayer for Walking

Lift my eyes, O God, from those things I see to the things I cannot see. Amen.

The Lord Is My Shepherd

The Lord is my shepherd, I shall not want. He makes me lie down in green pastures; he leads me beside still waters; he restores my soul. He leads me in right paths for his name's sake. Even though I walk through the darkest valley, I fear no evil; for you are with me; your rod and your staff—they comfort me. You prepare a table before me in the presence of my enemies; you anoint my head with oil; my cup overflows. Surely goodness and mercy shall follow me all the days of my life, and I shall dwell in the house of the Lord my whole life long. (Psalm 23)

It is an old and familiar psalm. We read it for comfort. We remember it for assurance. We recite it for confidence.

The Psalmist must have been a pilgrim. How else could he or she have recognized and called attention to all the places we walk? Green pastures, still waters, paths of righteousness, and valleys, the Psalmist speaks from the heart of a traveler, a walker.

The entire psalm is a poem of great beauty, but I particularly like the image of having my cup overflow. I use this metaphor on those rare and splendid moments when my heart is filled with overwhelming love and I am moved beyond words.

"My cup overflows," I say. And most everyone who hears those words seems to understand what they mean. It has become an image and an idea to which we hold dear.

When I, like the Psalmist, think about the goodness and mercy and shepherding of God, I sense my cup is overflowing, that I am filled up and running over with a sense of gratitude and humility.

Today as I walk, my heart spills from my eyes. My cup overflows.

Meditation for Walking

When was the last time your cup overflowed? Were you being attentive to the Shepherd when it occurred?

Prayer for Walking

As I walk along the path before me, Loving God, let me feel your guidance as a sheep feels the guidance of the shepherd. Amen.

What Is Required?

He has told you, O mortal, what is good; and what does the Lord require of you but to do justice, and to love kindness, and to walk humbly with your God? (Micah 6:8)

Walking humbly with God. There is action on our spiritual path. It is not a passive journey. We are told to walk humbly with our God. There is movement. Act. Love. Walk.

God does not call us to be immobile. God calls us to a life of service in the world, a service that includes love and justice and humility.

Many times people of faith think there is no require-ment in a life of servanthood. We think the expectations God has for us are minimal, if at all. We like to think we are free to do as we please. The prophet Micah, however, reminds us there are clear expectations that we are to live different lives from those who have no faith, expectations that we are to be active in the world, working for and showing love and justice. There is the expectation that as we move across the earth, across the path of life, we do so in humility with a God who walks and moves with us.

Action is required, but not a mad, chaotic action. We are not required to run or to image life as a marathon. It is easy to think that "walking" or even living a simple life of meet-ing these requirements is not enough. We are often con-vinced that only in running are we able to do any work for God's kingdom. And so we live in stages of running and exhaustion, running and exhaustion.

The prophet gives us a different model, a model of walking. When we envision ourselves walking with God, walking with purpose, to show love and justice, walking with a destination, back to the place where we all began, home, and walking in relationship with God and those around us, suddenly we find ourselves living much healthier and happier lives.

These prophetic words, however, were not spoken as a means to happiness but as a means to tell us what is required of mortals by God. That joy is the byproduct of living out these requirements is simply the gift we find when we slow down from our running and start to walk. From these words we discover the secret of how to live a life of faith: do justice, love kindness, and walk humbly with God.

Meditation for Walking

Do you exhibit the balance of walking in your life, or do you feel as if you alternate between inactivity and running? How would your life be different if you used this Scripture as your "guiding light"?

Prayer for Walking

In my lack of action, give me motion. In my need to run, slow me down. Let me walk humbly with you, Dear God. Amen.

Where the Seed Falls

A sower went out to sow his seed; and as he sowed, some fell on the path and was trampled on, and the birds of the air ate it up. Some fell on the rock; and as it grew up, it withered for lack of moisture. Some fell among thorns, and the thorns grew with it and choked it. Some fell into good soil, and when it grew, it produced a hundredfold. (Luke 8:5-8a)

Today I went over the entire finished part of the path. Sometimes I forge into new territory; sometimes, after storm and damage, I go back and start over, maintaining what already exists. Today in my raking I noticed something different. The types of soil change from one section of the path to another.

Some of it is rich and dark, loamy with earthworms, soft with the dust of old trees. Even though I have not walked across it barefooted, I know it is cold.

There is dry and rocky ground, sandy with pebbles. It tends to rise and be hilly. Nothing green threatens to grow here. Parts of the path that were thick with vines and still have undergrowth push through even where it has been cleared and raked. The earth is simply ripe there for vines and tangles.

There are passages that are easy to clear; the ground is solid. It is easy to push aside the leaves and straw. Underneath I discover an earth that can yield a great harvest. Good gardening soil, it seems, deep and close to a source of water.

I thought of this parable today as I walked from the scarred beginning of the path—how the earth seems to change in every way, even in color, how the ground rises and falls, curves and slides into the forest. I thought, as I paid attention, of all the places we travel in our lives on our spiritual paths. There are dry and lonely spells along with rich and easy places to pass. I thought of how likely I am to choose the easier way, only to discover I gained more from the rocky places, the more difficult passages.

Jesus explained his parable as pertaining to people who hear or don't hear the words of truth and what happens to the gospel depending upon the environment into which it passes. But I am drawn to other interpretations, other ideas regarding terrain.

Our paths cannot be across only one sort of soil. Our journey cannot take us through only one way of walking. We learn from the stones and the furrows, from the hidden roots that stumble us, and from the long, burdensome narrow passages. If our lives are noticed at all, we will discover we tread across a vast and various earth.

I have learned today to pay attention to the ground upon which I walk. I need to dress and journey accordingly, learning from all that is around me.

Meditation for Walking

Name the types of soil over which you have walked in your spiritual life. What did you learn from each terrain?

Prayer for Walking

Let me be aware, O God, of the soil upon which I pass this day. Let me learn from the places upon which I walk. Amen.

Week 38

Streams of Living Water

*Let the one who believes in me drink. As the scrip-
ture has said, "Out of the believer's heart shall
flow rivers of living water." (John 7:38)*

It was much too cold to walk or work on the path today.
Instead I stayed inside, visited with some of the home-
bound members of the church, and went with my husband
to take two children to a movie. As I read this passage from
the Gospel of John, I am struck by the verse. I claim belief
in Jesus, and yet I wonder about myself: "Do I have streams
of living water flowing from within me?"

One time as we drove along a country road, my mother
mentioned that there doesn't seem to be much moving
water. "Years ago," she said, "you never saw swampy, still
water like you do now. Water had a source, and from the
source it flowed, alive and clear."

I have heard others speak of drinking the cleanest
water fed to them by their hands, having dipped into a
stream or creek. The thought of such a thing is ludicrous
today since most of the creeks are heavily polluted, the
streams dried up. Drinking from a natural body of water is
a foreign idea to children today. Perhaps even the idea of
"living water" seems a bit outdated. Yet I am fortunate
because I still remember, still have seen streams of living
water.

I wonder about people of faith today. Have our lives
become stale like pools of swamp water? Have we lost the
connection with our source that keeps the water clean and
moving? Or have our streams become clogged with the
pollution of anger or self-absorption? Have we become
stagnant, cut-off, dried up, and muddy?

Jesus promised his disciples that others will recognize our faith by what flows freely in us; that through our relationship with him we experience living water, water that is alive and dancing, clear and clean. When I find myself muddied, stagnant, my faith like a swamp, I am reminded to go back to the source and see if new water won't flow from within me. Perhaps I have been standing in one place too long.

Meditation for Walking

Do you have a living relationship with Christ? What blocks living water from flowing within you?

Prayer for Walking

Living water, flow in me. Amen.

The Root Sustains You

But if some of the branches were broken off, and you, a wild olive shoot, were grafted in their place to share the rich root of the olive tree, do not boast over the branches. If you do boast, remember that it is not you that support the root, but the root that supports you. (Romans 11:17-18)

Arrogance is an easy attitude to take. The sense that I know better or best—that only I can do this activity, handle this project well—is so easily presumed that often we do not recognize it.

It's an interesting notion, me, a wild olive, grafted in among branches already existent. I can feel my leaves stretch, my fruit widen. I am healthier, more productive, and easier to maintain than the lopped-off branches near me.

Paul, of course, was speaking to the Gentiles who came to the faith after the Jews. In this verse to the Roman Church he reminds the new Christians that they must not make themselves superior. It's a great instruction, but it is so often and easily ignored.

When we are blooming, our fruit hearty and strong, it is a simple thing to notice dead and dried-up branches that exist so very near. In our bloom and heartiness it is tempting to look around and wonder why everyone else can't be as strong as we, desiring to call attention to the ripeness of our fruit, the color of our stems.

We are reminded, however, that we do not hold up the tree. We are not responsible for the entire plant. We do not sustain the root. The root sustains and holds up the branches, even and especially the wild olive that has been grafted. Part of the spiritual journey is to recognize our places in the order of things. We are not superior to anything or anyone. We are all sustained by our connection to the Creator. If our branches are strong, then we must give thanks to God because it is God who has granted us strength.

If we see something or someone who is dry and barren, let us not judge them or decide that we are better. Instead, let us bend as we are able to bring the branch back to its rootedness, and let us lend ourselves for their restoration. We dare not boast of our fruit or health. Our strength comes from the Lord.

Meditation for Walking

How does arrogance raise its ugly head in your life?
To what person or persons do you feel superior?

Prayer for Walking

When I boast, Dear God, let it only be of you. Amen.

Spring

signs of new life

Week 40

The Extra Day

So do not worry about tomorrow, for tomorrow will bring worries of its own. Today's trouble is enough for today. (Matthew 6:34)

February, the shortest month in the calendar year, is known as the month of love. Sometimes there is an extra day in this shortest month. When that happens, we call it "leap year." It means there is a 29th day, an additional 24 hours, all free, with no strings attached.

You know how we're always needing an extra hour to get things done? You know how we're always wishing for one more day in the week before that big paper is due or before that dreaded dentist appointment? Well, during leap year we have that gift of an extra day.

Typically, however, during leap year, when we get that day, we just fly right through it hardly recognizing it as a gift. It becomes just another Monday or Tuesday. More than likely, we will run late again, as usual. We're still out of milk. We're still needing to clean out that hall closet. More than likely, we spend that day like every other day, just trying to get through it. More than likely, this gift of a day will come and go, and no one will have noticed.

I began my ministry working with Hospice. It was in that experience that I began to understand the importance of February 29, the extra day. While working with folks who were terminally ill, I was challenged to recognize the gift of each day.

People who are dying have a way of making you see life through their eyes. And it's an incredible, unbelievable vision. There is a clarity of what's really important, what's really worth arguing about or fighting over, what needs to be said right now, how beautiful a sunrise can be. To a person who is dying, each day is a gift. While I worked with Hospice, I had to look at what I did with my days, how wisely or unwisely I spent them. I learned great lessons. Every leap year I am reminded of the gift of the extra day. And because February is the month of love, I am reminded to use that 29th day as a day of love.

Today as I walk this path remembering the gift of every day, the gift of love, the gift of life, I am able to release my anxiety about where the path has been or even where it is going. Today, regardless of the date, is the gift of the extra day. I shall be thankful for this day without worry or fear.

Meditation for Walking

If you had the gift of an extra day, how would you spend it? Can today be that day for you?

Prayer for Walking

Let me live today; let me love today, recognizing it as a gift. Amen.

The Lord Is Good

For the Lord is good; his steadfast love endures forever, and his faithfulness to all generations. (Psalm 100:5)

As I walk upon these fields of seed-strewn dust,
the golden earth, a mirror to the sun,
I think of myself as dancing.

loose from the lip of some tongue-tied angel
the cut of her eye daring me
to leap higher, deeper, longer.

I surprise even myself at the thought of such
formless prayer seeking no answer or structure—
only a wink to taste the ripe dawn
as it breaks about me.

I am the red breath of fire,
the flat space of sky,
the smoothness of newborn blooms,
bursting through thorns.
And I lean upon the whim of winds
without worry or need or definition.

Broken are the binding cords;
threadbare is the tangle of ropes
that lynch and choke.

Garbled are the reasons counting all costs,
the rules and logic
that cast my prints deep into a ground.

Today I have been unfolded
to the edge of this new morning.

The angel dips; I fall with a laugh,
tapping into the cadence of creation.
It is a whirl I faintly recognize
as I walk upon these fields.

Meditation for Walking

When was the last time you experienced "unfolding
to the edge of a new morning?" How did it feel to
realize the goodness of God?

Prayer for Walking

May my path speak of your goodness, O God. Let
me dance in you. Amen.

Taking the Way That Leads to Good

Thus says the Lord: Stand at the crossroads, and look, and ask for the ancient paths, where the good way lies; and walk in it, and find rest for your souls. (Jeremiah 6:16a)

Taking the way that leads to good sounds like such a simple idea. Of course, I will take the way that leads to good. Would I intentionally take a way that leads to evil? And yet, why does it seem so often that I take the wrong way? Was I not paying attention? Do I have self-destructive tendencies I have not noticed? Am I intrinsically evil and more prone to take that way?

I think not. I believe the secret to taking the way that leads to good comes in the suggestion before this sentence in the passage from Jeremiah. "Ask for the ancient paths, where the good way lies."

Knowing history and tradition and understanding the ways of our parents and grandparents and great-grand-parents can provide us with great courage and wisdom. Their choices and paths affect the choices we are called to make. Let us examine their ways, know the paths of others who seek to follow God's way. Let these walked-upon, crawled-upon paths inform the choices we make.

Notice also that God tells us to ask which is the way leading to good. It is not meant to be a haphazard guess, these paths we take. God has the information to pass on to us, if we are only willing to ask.

When I find myself walking on paths of evil, paths of destruction either for myself or others, paths where healing is not received, wholeness and purpose unfulfilled—it is chiefly because I have not stood and watched at the crossroads. I have been unable or unwilling to remember and learn from the paths of others. And for whatever reason—disbelief, impatience, self-hatred—I fail to ask God to show me the path that leads to goodness.

It seems to me that when I am at my worst, irritable and chaotic, miserable and unhappy in all things, it comes after ceaseless walking or running, a lengthy journey without a pause to stand and watch and remember and ask. And when I am at my best, gentle in spirit, believing in faith that all things shall be well, joyful in heart, it comes after I have had deliberate, or perhaps forced, moments of stillness and silence so that the request for a direction has been able to be articulated.

Perhaps as we journey on our paths we could hold this passage of Scripture in our hearts. It could only help us find the path of goodness.

Meditation for Walking

Think of a time when you stopped at a crossroads and carefully considered the paths of others and asked, "Which is the way that leads to good?" How did the situation work out? Compare it to a time when you rushed straight into a decision without this consideration. How were the outcomes different?

Prayer for Walking

As I walk today, let me know the way of goodness. Amen.

Not Busying Myself with Great Affairs

I do not busy myself with great affairs or things too marvelous for me. But I am calm and quiet like a weaned child clinging to its mother. (Psalm 131:1a, 2 RSV)

It is easy to miss the little things when we focus on issues or ideas that are grand. Sometimes, in fact, I completely overlook an answer because I am expecting something more marvelous than the one I received.

I am reminded of the story of Elijah waiting for God. There's an earthquake, a great wind, and fire, large and magnificent demonstrations of the power of God; but God is not in any of these demonstrations. God is in the still quiet voice that follows these great and violent displays.

In my living and on the path I uncover, I find myself so focused on the ending, the final product, the greater good, that I walk right over, look just beyond, push through the process or the daily happenings, the things just at my feet, that could teach me so much.

I am reminded by the Psalmist that a way to find hope in God, a restoration of my faith, is not found by busying myself with affairs that are too great or on marvelous things. But rather, calmness and quietness come when I focus on the moment, the breath, the patch of dirt I scratch, the event at hand.

The journey on our paths is meant to teach us many things. We must simply walk with open eyes to see that which is unfolding right before us.

Meditation for Walking

Spend today not busying yourself with great affairs. Focus on the little things.

Prayer for Walking

Teach me the calm and quiet ways of a child clinging to its mother. Amen.

The Source of Love Is God

Beloved, let us love one another, because love is from God; everyone who loves is born of God and knows God. Whoever does not love does not know God, for God is love. (1 John 4:7-8)

No matter where the path may take a person, it is and always will be, when it is a spiritual path, a path of love, a path that leads to love. That is the ultimate check point, the best litmus test for a direction, calling, or idea that claims to be of or from God. If this direction, calling, or idea does not speak of love, it is not of God.

If the path is moving one towards self-destructive behavior or harm towards others (including the earth and all creatures therein), then this is not the path of God's will. This path must be brought into the light of God's love, which will make clear the good or detriment into which the path is leading.

The writer of this letter in 1 John states clearly that the source of love is God. Therefore, all things that speak of love, call attention to love, or create love come from God. These can be things the world or church may not claim as religious things. But if we choose to believe these words of Scripture, then it matters not if these "things" have been justified by religious authority. In the same manner, if something or someone uses the language of religion or claims to be of God's agenda, but it is not an agenda, not a language grounded in love and points not to love, then it is only words and not of God's agenda.

As I walk along the path, going deeper into the forest, into the unknown, I ask myself the question, "Am I moving out of and into love?" If I cannot answer the question in the affirmative, then I have moved into the wrong direction.

Meditation for Walking

Is love the source and purpose of all you do? What is the source and purpose of the things that occupy your heart and mind?

Prayer for Walking

Always and only love. Amen.

The Art of Patience

To be patient shows great understanding; quick temper is the height of folly. (Proverbs 14:29 RSV)

Patience is not just some quality one finally attains like a finish line of a race. Patience is an endeavor, a lifelong venture for most people. Not merely a virtue, patience is a matter of changing focus. We move our sights away from the thing for which we wait and to the source of all things, God. If we are able to alter the focus in this way, we will find that patience is a natural outgrowth of our faith.

I am very close to being finished. I can see the orange marker that signals the far end of our property line. From here the path, now out of the woods, will simply move across a creek and into a meadow, where I will no longer "make" or even "uncover" the path.

The ground in this area is the hardest to clear. Perhaps because these plants grow near a source of water, their roots are tougher. It is more of a grassy area; few trees cover this section of the woods. Instead, many clumps of strong green growth and long yellow strands, like wheat, are found beneath two or three layers of leaves. It takes raking the leaves away first, then digging up the grass before the path begins to show itself. It is slow, arduous work that often forces me to stop and rest.

I am learning patience in my personal life while I wait for some word regarding publication of my first novel and the possibility of acceptance into school. Every day, no even every hour, I try to turn my focus away from the outcome, hearing some word, to God who shall hold me in the palm of God's hand regardless of the outcome.

Just as I struggle through this last section of my path and see the finish line but continue to make slow progress towards it, I attempt to focus not on the finish but rather on the Creator of the path, the one who showed me the idea, gave me the vision, nurtured it, sustained it, and brought me this far.

As long as I can keep my eyes directed on the source of the path, I need not be worried, anxious, or impatient regarding its outcome.

Meditation for Walking

Where in your life do you need patience? Are you able to shift the focus from the outcome or goal you await to God?

Prayer for Walking

And when I cannot wait another minute, O God, teach me how to make it for two. Amen.

Week 46

Walking the Path of Love

*All the paths of the Lord are steadfast love and
faithfulness, for those who keep his covenant and
his decrees. (Psalm 25:10)*

A creek divides the pine tree forest where the path began
from a cleared meadow just at the end of our property line.
The line is staked by a fence, one section of a very large
dairy farm. My husband cleared this meadow three years
ago, unsure of any plans for it.

This creek is not a moving body of water. It is more just
large puddles with stagnant water standing. But a bridge
must be built across it since the way would be too muddy
to walk. This will be the only place where I am not doing
the bulk of the work; my husband has agreed to cut and
gather the wood for the bridge. So, essentially I am finished
with the first uncovering of the path.

After working the area near the creek, I walked back to
the beginning, both beginnings, the original and the one
forced upon me after the tree-cutting incident. I dug out
the rocks I had found to mark it and took them to the new
starting place that has Saint Francis and an angel on the
two sides. I was surprised to find that the largest stone I
had previous acquired was, if turned in the appropriate
way, the shape of a crude but recognizable Valentine heart.
I had not seen it the first time I placed it in the ground. But
this time, now at the end of my path, it was quite clear. It
reminded me once again that no matter what direction or
terrain or pace our paths will travel, if it is the path of
God's will in our lives, it must always be measured with
love. God's path for our lives is always a path of love.

Funny, isn't it, that it took me traveling the entire path, building and unbuilding, working and looking for an answer, only to discover it had been there all along. I simply had to change the way I looked for answers.

The path I take, the path I seek to take, the path I uncover is the path of love.

Meditation for Walking

How can you be sure your path is a path of love?

Prayer for Walking

And when I walk straight from this world to the next, let me walk then as I attempt to walk now, into and out of your love. Amen.

Joy Comes with the Morning

Weeping may linger for the night, but joy comes with the morning. (Psalm 30:5b)

It is just before daylight, and I have left the warmth and safety of my bed to venture into the woods. Birds are beginning to wake. I hear the low rustle of animals looking for their morning food. But for now it is dark and mostly silent.

There have been nights that I thought would never end. There were nights when sorrow and disappointment and pain seemed as if they would capture the light of morning and keep my heart and spirit from knowing anything other than what it knew at that dark hour. In such an hour I found a familiar passage in the Psalms.

The psalmist knew the pain of a night of weeping. He understood what it was to be lost to the darkness. And yet, just as dawn comes to these shadowed woods, so shall the light of hope melt the midnight of sorrow. There may be hours of despair and seeing no way out, but morning always comes.

Perhaps, as I stand waiting for the light of dawn, the Psalmist stood also in the pitch of night, unsure that light would come, but confident in the love of a God who promises us relief. Perhaps these words were written before the joy of morning had reassured him. But even in the weeping of the long, dark night, somehow he knew what I know as I stand waiting to be able to see. Morning will come. Dawn will break. Joy will take the place of weeping.

Meditation for Walking

Ponder the words of Scripture. Meditate upon the joy that awaits.

Prayer for Walking

Remind me, ensure me, O God, weeping may last the night; but joy will come in the morning. Amen.

Keep Going

And let us consider how to provoke one another to love and good deeds, not neglecting to meet together, as is the habit of some, but encouraging one another, and all the more as you see the Day approaching. (Hebrews 10:24-25)

"Kim and Todd, Keep Going." These were the words written on a poster nailed to the stop sign at a crossroads near my house. I'm sure it was meant for some people who were trying to get to a party or to a friend's home. The sign was merely information regarding a map and directions. But as I turned the corner, I thought, "What a wonderful road sign upon which to come." And I began to wonder about Kim and Todd.

They could have been brother and sister or just friends traveling together. But I imagine them as a couple, and more than likely, city folk. My guess is that their host knew they would feel lost, stuck on a country road. So the sign was meant to encourage them, let them know they were heading in the right direction. They were not forgotten or alone.

If your sense of direction is anything like mine, then you have spent many occasions feeling lost on country roads and along city bypasses. They are not occasions I particularly enjoy. Yet, doesn't it feel good when you finally recognize a landmark or figure out how to get where you're going? For me, it's a feeling of great relief and peace to know, at last, I am where I'm supposed to be.

It's no different as we walk along our spiritual paths. There are times when we lose our sense of direction and become confused about where we are. Finding signs of encouragement and familiarity are like guardian angels perched above the unclear road signs, letting us know in confidence that we're headed in the right way. Sometimes those signs of encouragement are found in Scripture. Sometimes those signs are discovered from the text of a sermon or prayer in worship. But sometimes those signs are the gifts we give to one another in the form of love and support by saying, "My friend, keep going."

The author of the letter to the Hebrews reminds us that it is part of our responsibility as pilgrims on this path to encourage and support one another. Let us share expressions of hope to each other.

Meditation for Walking

What signs of encouragement have you known along your path? What sign can you share with others this week?

Prayer for Walking

Let my life be a sign of hope to others. Amen.

And She Praised God

There appeared a woman with a spirit that had crippled her for eighteen years. She was bent over and quite unable to stand up straight. When he laid his hands on her, immediately she stood up straight and began praising God. (Luke 13:11, 13)

Time passes so slowly
when your face is to the ground.

Eyes catching sunlight
only in the stones
that gather in the streets.

Seeing humanity only tied in thongs
Sandals clutching souls.

My face longs to feel the wind's breath
as it stirs within my hair.
My arms ache to reach out
to clasp my sister's face to kiss;
my body crouched so tightly
into this life called "woman."

What holy day could today be?

Do I dare believe that today I might dance?
Do I dare dream that today
someone shall call out my name, "WOMAN?"

my feet to jump
my eyes to focus heavenward
my arms to reach out
one towards the mountains
the other to touch freedom
as it lies buried in your smile

Do I dare believe?

Time passes so slowly
when your face is to the ground.

Meditation for Walking

What have you chosen not to believe because your
eyes cannot be lifted?

Prayer for Walking

God of grace, God of glory, let me dare to dream.
Amen.

The Light of Life

Again Jesus spoke to them, saying, "I am the light of the world. Whoever follows me will never walk in darkness but will have the light of life." (John 8:12)

A light bulb has gone out in our bathroom. At first the reduced amount of light was very noticeable. I intended for a number of days to replace the bulb. I expected my husband would at some point replace the bulb. Neither of us has done so, and now it's been a number of weeks since the bulb has gone out. I have grown accustomed to the room without as much light as is intended.

It's interesting what we get used to in our lives. If we allow ourselves to listen to negative talk long enough, we begin to accept that negativity as reality. If we permit ourselves to be beaten down long enough, we begin to walk in a posture of submissiveness. If we walk a path in darkness long enough, we begin to lose any expectation of receiving light.

In the Gospel of John Jesus tells his followers that he has come that we might walk with the light of life, that we are not meant to walk in darkness. We are not meant to become accustomed to living without light.

When I walk the path at night, things become unclear. I stumble. I lose my way. I cannot remember nor see the guideposts set along the path. As I grope along in the darkness, even upon a path that has become familiar to me, I embrace these words of Jesus and decide not to walk in darkness any longer. The light shall not be taken from me. I walk as a child of God. I walk as a person of light. I journey unwilling to believe that I am to walk any other way.

An earthworm emerges from beneath the dark, wet ground. Pink and long, he struggles to get back to his comfortable depth. How blinding is the light when we are so accustomed to the darkness.

Meditation for Walking

Where has the light gone out in your life?

Prayer for Walking

God of light, lead me from the darkness into the light. Amen.

Week 51

The Path of Life

You show me the path of life. In your presence there is fullness of joy; in your right hand are pleasures forevermore. (Psalms 16:11)

The bridge is complete. The path is ready to be walked. A group of ministers will be coming at the start of Holy Week to take the passage and have a time of meditation.

It is a little unnerving to think about sharing this very personal journey with others, allowing friends to see what has been uncovered in this process. But it also is time to share, for I believe there is much to be experienced from this walk in the woods. Any time we slow down to listen and observe, we will be blessed. A part of our journey is sharing those blessings with one another.

As I walk along this path and remember the days, good and bad, from start to finish, I am fully aware that God intends our paths to be . . .

> paths of life, not death
> > paths of love, not hate
> > > paths of joy, not sorrow
> > > > paths of goodness, not evil.

At times we must tarry through difficulties, but sometimes it is enough to carry us through, just to understand the intention of God: to be created in God's image and walk along paths of goodness and life. I share this path in faith that God will bless the journey of another.

109

Meditation for Walking

What will you share about your path with others?

Prayer for Walking

Holy God, walk with me this day that I may bear witness to your path of life. Amen.

Week 52

Benedictions

*The grace of the Lord Jesus Christ, the love of God,
and the communion of the Holy Spirit be with all
of you. (2 Corinthians 13:13)*

One of my favorite activities as a pastor is the act of delivering the benediction. It was my first "official" act as an ordained minister, so it always brings a certain amount of nostalgia to the action. And there is pleasure in having the last word. But regardless of why I enjoy offering the blessing, I respect the opportunity and attempt to offer it by and through God's grace.

I use the benediction to remind the congregation that nothing shall come across their path in the weeks or months or lifetime ahead of them that shall separate them from the love of God. There shall be no evil nor tragedy nor crisis that can take away their foundation. For since we are a people of faith, our foundation is built upon a solid rock. And because of that rock, we have all the resources we need to weather any storm, handle any problem.

Hear now, pilgrim of faith, a benediction for you as you make your journey.

*My friend as you walk your path, hold fast to the
knowledge that nothing shall separate you from
the goodness of God. No evil, no memory, no event
or circumstance, no person, no thing, no loss, no
crisis, no trouble. For you are sustained through
God's love, the grace of Christ Jesus, the fellowship
and communion of the Holy Spirit, and the love
of other pilgrims who walk near and with you.
With this knowledge and sustenance you can be
confident that you are able to walk in peace.*

Meditation for Walking

What blessing do you need to hear as you walk your path?

Prayer for Walking

Relying upon the resources of God's love and grace and the gifts of God's son and the Holy Spirit, let me walk in peace. Amen.